THE REAL WORLD OF
BEATRIX POTTER

by
ELIZABETH BATTRICK

INTRODUCTION

Elizabeth Battrick first had the idea of writing this book when researching an article on the revival, between the wars, of country dancing in Westmorland. She was surprised to find that Mrs William Heelis, née Beatrix Potter, had taken a great interest in the Sawrey Country Dancing Team led by her husband, going with them to country dancing evenings in village halls and the upper rooms of country pubs. This glimpse of Beatrix Potter's married life, so different from the preceding long years of supervising the management of No. 2 Bolton Gardens, and waiting in dutiful attendance on her parents, made Mrs Battrick realise that, after her marriage, Beatrix Potter had moved into a different world.

She found several people still living in Sawrey who had known Beatrix Potter and were happy to share their memories. In particular Tom Storey, who could recall almost verbatim some of the exchanges between Mrs Heelis and himself. Then National Trust dead files yielded letters from the period when Mrs Heelis managed Monk Coniston properties for the Trust. The story of the fulfilling years began to unfold.

The resulting book outlines the support given by Mrs Heelis to the National Trust and the influence she had on forming the Trust's present farming policy. It is also a picture of a woman who achieved her ambition to live, be accepted and have some part in protecting the countryside and way of life she loved.

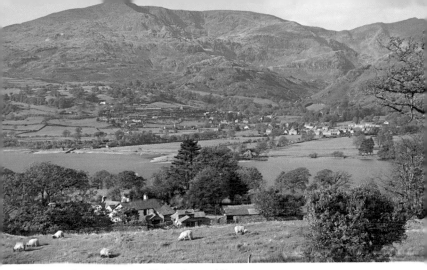

'The most pleasant countryside in the world'

THE REAL WORLD OF BEATRIX POTTER

On a fine autumn day in September 1937, when she was seventy-one years old, Mrs William Heelis drove up to Heathwaite Farm below the Old Man of Coniston in a milk float, taking the reins herself. She was to lunch with Delmar and Josephine Banner, two young artist friends. Her old car, a black and green Talbot which she had nicknamed 'Noah's Ark', was beyond getting up the hill, so they had provided a horse-drawn vehicle instead with a plank and their willing hands to help her mount.

Walter the chauffeur was left with the car at Church Bridge in the village, Mrs Heelis chirruped to the horse and gathered in the reins, the two young people trotted, one on each side of the float, and the journey became a sort of royal progress, with handkerchiefs waved from every cottage win-

The gentle hills at 'back o't lake'

dow and autumn cottage flowers sent up in advance to be arranged and ready in the best parlour. For lunch, cooked by the farmer's wife, there was a roast of lamb with peas followed by a plum tart, all of which Mrs Heelis enjoyed.

After the lunch Mrs Heelis inspected the shippons (cattle sheds) and Delmar's paintings, both of them with a professional eye, then took the reins to drive back down the hill. She had bought a view of Coniston Fells from Hardknott Pass, in which she considered the clouds were wonderful, and she advised Delmar to study trees. She thought they were, in their right place, as beautiful as lakes and had a nobility of growth which was seriously overlooked.

Castle Cottage

Mrs Heelis no longer painted; her eyes were not up to it, and in fact the room she had made at Hill Top for writing and painting, where she had hung pictures by her brother Bertram, had hardly seen her since 1913. Her marriage and her interest in farming had filled her life from then on. In 1937 Mrs Heelis thought of herself entirely as a farmer; the years of creation had been satisfactory, but were not now important.

It was late in the afternoon when the milk float, with the two young artists breathless beside it, arrived back in Coniston village. Walter the chauffeur stood by the old Talbot as disapproving as usual as he preferred horses to

Portrait of Beatrix Potter by Delmar Banner

cars, having been groom to Mrs Heelis's late mother until
she died. After farewells were said he drove Mrs Heelis back
from Coniston to Castle Cottage in Near Sawrey, her home
for twenty-four years. At seventy-one Mrs Heelis had bril-
liant blue eyes, rosy cheeks and silky white hair that was
parted in the middle and brought to a small bun at the nape
of her neck. It was kept in place by a velvet ribbon tied with

a little bow on the top of her head. She wore comfortable country clothes and was altogether as neat and tidy and bright-eyed as one of her own little housewifely animal characters – perhaps Mrs Tiggy-Winkle. 'She was a bonny woman; she stayed bonny all her life,' her shepherd, Tom Storey, was to say years later. Talking to her, Josephine was to observe in time to come, was like eating brown bread after having never tasted anything but white.

Walter would have gone home to the Old Post Office where he and his wife lived as tenants of his employer, and Mrs Heelis would have put her husband's slippers to warm,

Below: *Tom Storey among his 'favourite' sheep*
Following page: *A landscape in need of protection*

laid a white cloth on the table and lit the candles ready for his return. Drawing the curtains she would have looked across the field in the direction of Hill Top, just a field away, which had inspired so many of her books.

The start of her real life twenty-four years before must have seemed a long way in the past when, a few days after the lunch at Heathwaite, Mrs Heelis wrote to thank Mr and Mrs Delmar Banner for their hospitality – and transport – and her private view of the pictures. The spontaneous welcome she had received, both on her journey and at the Banners', showing with what affection and respect she was regarded in her adopted country, must have brought home to her how thoroughly she had become an accepted part of the very real world of the Lake District – how very far behind her was her curious life as Miss Beatrix Potter at No. 2 Bolton Gardens in London.

As a girl and a young woman Beatrix Potter had been expected by her parents to remain mostly in the schoolroom at the top of the house. In the early years her brother Bertram had kept her company, but he was soon sent away to school. This left Beatrix with only the companionship of her various governesses and her animals. Smuggled into the house in muffs and handbags, mice, rabbits and hedgehogs remained, she found, delightfully themselves regardless of their environment. Her mother's life consisted of interviewing the cook after breakfast, writing little notes and driving out to make calls after lunch. Her father, as a result of her grandfather being a Manchester man who had built up a most successful calico-printing business, was able to spend much of his time at his club.

Wray Castle from the lake

Every summer there was a welcome break in the routine when the Potter family went on a three-month holiday, during which the yearly house-cleaning was undertaken at Bolton Gardens. Mr and Mrs Potter, both being of north country origin, often chose to visit either Scotland or the Lake District, taking a large furnished country house in which their servants were expected to re-create the routine of the London home. Outside, however, there was the countryside to explore, fresh air and freedom for both children for a few weeks and an opportunity for Mr Potter to indulge his hobby of photography.

Wray Castle, on the west shore of Windermere, was first discovered as an ideal holiday residence by Mr Potter when Beatrix was in her mid teens. The castle was in fact a

Hardwicke Rawnsley with Beatrix and her father at Wray

Victorian folly, with seven reception rooms and mock ruins which were supposed to frame the view of the lake, and it amused Beatrix to record in her diary that it was built by a Dr Dawson with his wife's money, though she never lived there – and the architect drank himself to death before the house was finished. Around this gloomy mansion, though, there was pleasant rolling countryside which Beatrix came to know and love, and it was because they stayed at Wray that Hardwicke Rawnsley came into their lives.

Hardwicke Drummond Rawnsley was at that time the Vicar of Wray, his first living. He was also something of a literary figure, having published a book on Egypt, and it was in this capacity he was consulted by Rupert Potter, who was looking for advice on his new hobby of collecting autographed letters of the Lake Poets. Hardwicke's warm personality and knowledge of the countryside soon made him a welcome visitor to the castle.

Hardwicke, too, had hobbies and enthusiasms; an incurable habit of writing impromptu verse to fit every occasion, a delight in dialect speech and a hatred of anything that threat-

The original Peter Rabbit drawn by Beatrix Potter in 1898
© *Frederick Warne & Co., 1980*

ened his beloved Lake District, especially expanding railway companies. He had an extraordinary idea, too, for forming a holding company for beautiful countryside saved from the developer by money raised by public subscription. His whirl-wind energy encompassed his friends, demanding their involvement in his concerns, but he also took the greatest pleasure in hearing about other people's interests and help-ing wherever he could. The habitual reserve Beatrix wrapped about herself was quite melted by Hardwicke's interest in her animals – she took them with her on holiday in small hutch-es and boxes – and by his loudly voiced opinion that her paintings were really good, quite worthy of encouragement. Until then no one had thought them more than a very suit-able occupation for a young lady.

The Potters returned frequently to the far side of Windermere 'back o't lake' as it was called, often staying in a house in Near Sawrey, Lake Field. Beatrix came to know the countryside well, going about sometimes sketching the vil-lage, sometimes driving her pony and phaeton, and keeping up the friendship with Hardwicke Rawnsley that continued until he died in 1920.

In London, Beatrix continued on her quiet way, caught up in a rigid routine of duty to her parents, responsibility for the running of the household, and the thought of a life of her own hardly to be considered. She continued to sketch, too, and when she was twenty-seven she illustrated a small book of verses for children. She also began to write about her ani-mals in letters to the children of a former governess. They seemed to enjoy both the sketches and the stories, so in her mid thirties Beatrix Potter considered publishing a little book called *The Tale of Peter Rabbit* and naturally asked Hardwicke Rawnsley for advice.

Hardwicke liked the drawings but thought the book would be improved if verse – his verse – was substituted for the prose narrative. He did in fact write a poetic version of *Peter Rabbit* which he carefully made up into a little book for her consideration.

> There were four little bunnies, no bunnies were
>   sweeter,
> Mopsy and Cotton-tail, Flopsy and Peter.
> They lived in a sand-bank, as here you may see
> At the foot of a fir   a magnificent tree.

In spite of Hardwicke's efforts, Beatrix had a preference for her own prose style, but she took some of his advice and offered her book to the publishing firm of Frederick Warne & Co. In the first place they did not accept the book, but swiftly changed their minds after Beatrix had it privately printed in 1900, and it sold extremely well. Warnes, particularly Norman Warne, encouraged her to write more books in the following four years – *Squirrel Nutkin*, *The Tailor of Gloucester* and *Benjamin Bunny*. The royalties from her little books, together with a small legacy, made it possible for her to buy Hill Top farm. From that moment on, Beatrix belonged to the Lake District, and her involvement with its people and its concerns was to grow deeper and deeper throughout her life.

The Potters were taking their long summer holiday in Near Sawrey when Hill Top farm came up for sale. Beatrix already knew it well, as Mr Beckett, the Potters' coachman,

Previous page: *Near Sawrey*. Above: *Hill Top*

his wife and two boys always had rooms at Hill Top when the family stayed at Lake Field. She realised it was exactly what she wanted – a small manageable farm where she could learn to be a farmer – in exactly the place she wanted – 'the most pleasant countryside in the world' – and she bought it at auction. It was represented to her parents as an investment and accepted as exactly that, but when Beatrix decided the tenant farmer in residence, John Cannon, should stay on, she also decided to build an extension to the farm for him and his family, so she could keep the old seventeenth-century house for her own use whenever she was able to visit it. She was to find the work of planning the extension, re-roofing the dairy, getting rid of the rats and decorating to be her one comfort in a desolate winter. Norman Warne, who had asked her to marry him and been joyfully accepted, though the engagement had been steadfastly ignored by her parents, died in August of pernicious anaemia.

Norman Warne had steadily and helpfully encouraged Beatrix in the writing of books for children, and after his death she felt those already completed and the planning of new ones to be the only satisfactory thing left in her life. In the following eight years she was to write thirteen successful books of which many were concerned with Hill Top and Sawrey. This was a remarkable achievement, as she was still expected to be the dutiful daughter of the house and for three-quarters of the year was either in London or paying a round of visits with a mother yearly more querulous and a father whose health was steadily failing. Even when her parents were safely established in a house within reach of Sawrey – the long summer holiday was now always in the Lake District – Beatrix could only get to Hill Top about four days in a week and, though she usually managed to catch the Coniston coach to get there, she often had a long walk back.

The time spent at Hill Top was full of delight. She was learning to be a farmer, to manage the straw-chopping machine and shake out the hay. She was always sketching the house, garden, countryside and animals for new books. Tom Kitten belonged to Mrs Cannon, Jemima Puddle-Duck too, and a great trial she had been to the farmer's wife. The General Shop in the village was the perfect background for *Ginger and Pickles*. The pleasure Beatrix Potter took in the realities of life in Sawrey can be seen in the loving observation of particular details in her books. Kep, in *Jemima Puddle-Duck*, went to look for two foxhound puppies who

The Ginger and Pickles shop. From The Tale of Ginger and Pickles,
© Frederick Warne & Co., 1909

were out at walk with the butcher. In *The Pie and the Patty-Pan* Beatrix had the cat Ribby observe how very comfortable the veal and ham pie looked cooking in the oven. Mrs Tiggy-Winkle, that admirable laundress, made up her kitchen fire

Jemima Puddle-Duck in Hill Top farmyard from The Tale of Jemima Puddle-Duck, *© Frederick Warne & Co., 1908*

with turf and hid the key under the door-sill. Mrs Tittlemouse, a much disturbed housewife, slept in a little box-bed.

The reactions were those of Sawrey when upsetting things

happened to her characters. Mrs Tabitha Twitchet was 'affronted' when she found her kittens with no clothes on; Mrs Tittlemouse, after her uninvited visitors the bees had gone, began a spring-cleaning that lasted a fortnight. When Tommy Brock snatched the Flopsy bunnies, their mother had taken away old Mr Bouncer's pipe and hidden his tobacco before having a complete spring-clean to relieve her feelings. The two villains, Tommy Brock and Mr Tod, were waiting for each other to die. During her farming years Mrs Heelis was to have a strong disagreement with a neighbour over the sale of a piece of land. 'We're like Mr Tod and Tommy Brock,' she said to a friend, 'just waiting . . .'.

Beatrix bought many pieces of land and property in and around Sawrey, first to increase the holding of Hill Top and later to save from demolition or unsuitable use such buildings as the Old Post Office, Castle Cottage and a number of small farms. In this she was influenced by Canon Rawnsley – he was made a Canon of Carlisle in 1909 – who was now not only Vicar of Crosthwaite in Keswick but was also the Honorary Secretary of the holding company for land and historic houses. It was called the National Trust.

The first property acquired for the Trust in the Lake District was Brandelhow Woods on Derwentwater, followed by Gowborrow Park on Ullswater and then Queen Adelaide's Hill on Windermere. The Canon appealed to all his friends for money for these projects as a matter of course, and Beatrix did not escape his persuasive scrawls. When he wrote to her about the Adelaide appeal she promised him a small subscription when she had been paid for a ham.

Even in 1913, when Beatrix had owned Hill Top for eight

years, was forty-seven years old and had received wide acclaim for her books, she found it difficult to leave her parents and stay there for any great length of time. She told Canon Rawnsley that a nurse had been engaged for her father, so sometimes she was able to stay at Hill Top for a night, but all in all it was difficult to get away.

Hardwicke had asked her for some information about a right of way that was being closed as the farmer could no longer put up with gates being left open and stock straying. Beatrix was of the opinion it was a pity to hear of visitors being turned back from fell land. As a farmer she felt they did less damage on the fells than in the valleys, where she had lately seen a party of large young women steeple chasing

Previous page: Brandelhow Old Park, Catbells, photographed by Rupert Potter
Below: Houses in Hawkshead given to the Trust by Beatrix Potter

Tabitha Twitchit's shop. From The Tale of the Pie and the Patty-Pan,
© *Frederick Warne & Co., 1905*

over a succession of newly 'cammed' walls in pursuit of
mushrooms. The trouble was they did not always shut gates
on coming down. She had a theory that self-shutting gates
might be the answer; there were some she had seen in Wales
worked with a log that might do the job.

She thought as a farmer, she looked on herself as a
farmer, but she had very little opportunity actually to be a
farmer. Her life, however, was soon to change. In 1909 she
had bought a bigger property, Castle Farm, in order to add
its fields to Hill Top. The firm of solicitors through whom
she made the purchase were W. Heelis & Co., and after the
transaction was completed one of the partners, William

Heelis, continued to take an interest in the affairs of this lady farmer who owned much of Sawrey but perforce spent a lot of her time away. He kept an eye on the various farms and cottages for her and when she was at Hill Top came to call, a tall distinguished country gentleman with a very dashing motorbicycle – a Bradbury with a basket-work side-car – which he left in the top entrance to the farm. The village was therefore not surprised when the engagement was announced, but Beatrix had great trouble with her parents who thought a country solicitor much beneath her.

View from Queen Adelaide's Hill

Fortunately her brother Bertram came to her rescue, announcing on one of his infrequent visits to London from his farm near Jedburgh that he had married a farmer's daughter years ago and was very happy – Beatrix had every right, at forty-seven, to marry whom she pleased. The opposition did not entirely disappear, going underground and threatening to break out every so often, but the marriage took place in Kensington in October 1913.

The honeymoon was spent in a furnished bungalow in Sawrey while Castle Cottage was refurbished for them. Hill Top was to be kept as it was; it was too small and primitive for the married couple, and Beatrix could not bear to change the house that had given her the opportunity to start to live a real life. It would be kept aired and dusted by Mrs Cannon, and Beatrix was to continue to look after the garden.

Two weeks after the marriage, Mrs Potter was changing servants and summoned Beatrix to London to be on hand to instruct the new parlour-maid. William came to fetch her after a few days; Mrs Heelis should be where she belonged, in Sawrey.

In 1937 farming was recovering from the Depression, and sheep and wool sales were bringing a little cheer to hill farmers at last. It had been a different matter when Mrs Heelis first came to live at Castle Cottage. The First World War overtook the newly married couple almost before they had time to turn round, and soon Mrs Heelis found herself working out in the fields with the few men left. Then Mr Potter died, and Mrs Potter spent most of the war in a furnished house in Windermere, having finally decided after the Armistice to come and live near her daughter. Lindeth

28

Above: *1922 Hawkshead Show Committee – Beatrix Potter, centre*
Following page: *Cockshot Point from the lake*

Howe, near the ferry in Windermere, was purchased, and it took Mrs Heelis two months to move her mother's possessions from No. 2 Bolton Gardens and settle her in her new home. Bertram had died suddenly in 1918; a great grief both to his mother and Beatrix.

After the four sad years of unremitting work were over, Mrs Heelis the farmer saw years of peace stretching ahead in which she could practise husbandry as she wished. She had other interests, too. One of them was dancing.

The folk-dancing revival of the twenties, which took Lake District villages by storm, met with the approval of

Mrs Heelis. She had long realised that old traditions of the countryside were dying – in 1911 she had persuaded the Sawrey 'Jolly Boys' to perform their pace-egging play in Hill Top garden so she could photograph this disappearing custom – so a revival of traditional folk-dancing was to be encouraged. William caught her enthusiasm and took to dancing himself, and transported members of the team, packed into his new Morris Cowley, to different villages. Mrs Heelis watched the dancing in stone-flagged kitchens – the Boatman, Black Nog – and over the store at Chapel Stile to the sound of Morris bells and the taste of plum cake. Then there were long – certainly cold – drives home in winter frost under bright stars with the dancers wrapped in rugs and packed into the dickie-seat. William was a careful driver.

The rehearsing was done in the Tower Bank Arms, near Hill Top. There was an old walnut piano in the kitchen where Margaret Burns, wife of the proprietor, would play for them. Mrs Heelis made the dresses for the Grasmere Folk Festival which they entered; a very pretty floral pink print.

Mrs Heelis had not lost interest in acquiring property either; quite the contrary. William had every opportunity as a local solicitor to know in advance when cottages or land were to be put up for sale – and there were many large estates being broken up in the years after the war, with apprehensive cottagers wondering who was to buy. Mrs Heelis bought where and when she could, always with an eye to preventing jerry-built bungalows swamping the villages and traditional cottages being demolished. Would-be makers of quick profits sometimes found themselves unexpectedly defeated.

Canon Rawnsley had died in 1920, full of years and honours and a fighter to the last for the preservation of the Lake District landscape. His greatest memorial was the National Trust, which was having increasing success in the protection of beautiful countryside. Mrs Heelis had come to think that the Canon was right in believing the Trust was the best hope for those who wanted to protect the land; large land-owners could go suddenly bankrupt or gamble their land away; smallholders, as she once complained to Mrs Rawnsley, stripped their land of all assets and then took to keeping hens.

Hardwicke Rawnsley had shouted his convictions from the rooftops and had talked and written widely about his successes and failures. Mrs Heelis preferred to be quiet, mouselike, about her aims and ambitions. She subscribed to Trust Appeals – now without the Canon to remind her – but anonymously, so the secret of how much she really gave to the Trust has never been told. She bought property discreetly, so few knew the sum total of her holdings; certainly not the village.

Sawrey, both Far and Near, thought they knew a lot about her. She liked porridge, she was devoted to William and she was the one who made decisions. William was greatly respected though, as a quiet gentleman and a good shot over rough land. They also knew her mother came up from Windermere to see her every Wednesday afternoon. Sawrey curtains twitched on Wednesdays.

Harry Byers, whose first job after he left school in 1916 was at Hill Top farm, saw the spectacle many times. 'Her mother visited every week,' he described it, 'coming over the ferry in the afternoon in her brougham. Mr Beckett, the coachman with top hat and cockade, would be driving the two horses, and Mr Stevens the groom hanging on the back. She always wore black, and I never saw her smile. She would stay exactly one hour and then she went back to Lindeth Howe.'

The villagers knew Mrs Heelis was an author as her books were for sale in the Ginger and Pickles shop. After she wrote *Ginger and Pickles*, the village store, smelling of yeast and bacon and disinfectant, was never called anything else – but they managed to put this at the back of their minds most of the time. After all, they were very *little* books. Mostly the villagers took her as they found her, an eccentric farmer (and employer) who wore clogs and a sacking apron and was even known to have covered her head with a rhubarb leaf in a hot hayfield.

They also knew her as someone who did not mince words. They had all heard the tale about her falling out with a neighbour whose sheep had strayed onto her fields. The old blacksmith had been there listening to it all. She really did give him something to be going on with, the blacksmith had said. She had got back almost as good as she gave, so then she put him in a book. There was also the tiresome habit she had of buying up a cottage that might have made a good gift shop or fish-and-chip emporium to tempt the trippers, but on the other hand if you needed a cottage unexpectedly for a daughter to be married, or for a widowed mother, Mrs Heelis might just be able to help.

People were to continue to ask her for help with their house-hunting problems. Her artist friends the Banners very much wanted a house – with a good view. 'I've some labourers' cottages, but I'll not let you have one of them,' she told them, jealously guarding the structure of village life. Later she heard of an estate being broken up near Elterwater and with her usual practical kindness wrote to tell them of a possible property in Great Langdale with good views, though she warned them of the dangers of living in remote places, with no road for coal carts. In the end Josephine and Delmar found their own house, a seventeenth-century farmhouse with the traditional built in carved cupboard and oak refectory table as well as a view. Considering the matter in later years Delmar felt sure that if Mrs Heelis had known the house was on the market before they did, she would have bought it in order to protect it – and then put them in as tenants. She was particularly interested in preserving intact the hand-carved panelling and furniture which used to be found in most farmhouses and cottages.

In turn, Mrs Heelis knew quite a lot about the village: those who over-indulged in Alexander's beer at the Tower Bank Arms, the difficulties when Jim Airey's bus, which plied between Hawkshead and the ferry and Ambleside – 2d. from Sawrey to Hawkshead   broke down. She was also familiar with the problems of illness in the cottages. There were always the usual epidemics of measles, mumps, whooping cough and scarlet fever, with visitations of flu and tuberculosis being quite common. Doctors were scarce and cost money; mostly people worried through as best they could. Mrs Heelis decided the villages needed a district nurse.

The Hawkshead and District Nursing Association was almost certainly her own creation. She happened to have a cottage just outside Hawkshead that would do nicely for the

Previous page: *Coniston Water.* Above: *The Tower Bank Arms*

nurse to live in, rent free and – the distances round
Hawkshead and the Sawreys being too great for a bicycle –
she dipped into her own pocket to buy a car. At the handing-
over ceremony Mrs Heelis planted a magnolia tree in the
cottage garden that has grown and flourished, as did the
rural medical services. The early system was simple. The
nurse called every day at Castle Cottage, and Mrs Heelis,
who knew or was kept informed of everyone who was ill,
gave her a daily list of visits. A further bonus was a Hill Top
turkey every Christmas.

It was farming, though, which stood at the centre of Mrs

Heelis's life. John Cannon retired at the end of the war, and William Mackereth from Grasmere came to Hill Top as manager. Mrs Heelis went up to the farm every day, taking a hand with this job or that, staying with a calving cow through the night in a cold byre, helping with haymaking and the harvest of oats. She began to take a greater interest in sheep, too, and learnt the art of training sheep dogs.

In 1924 another farm was added to the estate – Troutbeck Park Farm in the Troutbeck Valley near Windermere: a big farm this time, with fell grazing over hundreds of acres at heights up to 2,000 feet (610 m), plenty of bottom land and rich in history, but otherwise in a poor state.

In the year she bought Troutbeck Park Farm Mrs Heelis told a neighbour that when she followed the Coniston Hunt over Troutbeck Park land, she had had to take off her shoes and stockings and wade through a swollen beck, which she thought to be the only clean place on the farm. Tom Storey had the same opinion. 'It wasn't much when she took it. It was rotten with sheep fluke too. The lambs used to die like flies.'

The farm, however, was at the head of a dale with land tempting to developers and in need of protection. When improved it would be good for Herdwick sheep. This local breed, small, sure-footed as chamois and hardy above the average, had become an overriding interest. Their origin was obscure but they were able to live at higher altitudes and survive through blizzards better than any other breed. Their ability to know their own fell, to be 'heafed' to their own farm without the need for walls or fences, made them invaluable on the scarcely economic hill farms.

Mrs Heelis had started to breed a few at Hill Top with the idea of putting them into the autumn agricultural shows, but William Mackereth was not a sheep man and his efforts had not met with success. This state of affairs was not to her liking, and discreet enquiries were made. On a November afternoon in 1926 Mrs Heelis turned up outside the shippon at Townend Farm in Troutbeck.

'We'd just finished milking and my boss, he said, "There's a lady wants to see you,"' relates Tom Storey, 'and she came through the shippon door and – Mrs Heelis, she looked – well, a bonny looking woman to tell you the truth. "I've come to see you about working for me," she said. "Will you come to Troutbeck Park to be my shepherd?" I said yes if the money was right, and she offered me double what I was getting from the Greggs so that's how I got my start.'

Left: *Troutbeck Park Farm*. Below: *Herdwick sheep*

Previous pages; *Tilberthwaite Farm*
Left: *Winter privations*
Above: *Winter fells*

45

Tom Storey did well that first winter. A remedy against fluke worm had just come on the market, and Mrs Heelis agreed Tom should try it. 'She was always very good at sending for new cures, nothing was too good for the sheep.' So Tom successfully lambed 1,000 sheep and – 'Oh, she was set up.'

After that, nothing would suit Mrs Heelis but that Tom – William Mackereth having retired – should come to manage Hill Top farm to breed Herdwicks. There was one moment of disagreement when Tom moved in. He found several sheep 'put aside' with redded fleeces for showing. In Tom's opinion they were no good to show but Mrs Heelis thought differently. 'She was quite cut up about it. I didn't let her carry on. "If you want these sheep showing, Mrs Heelis, you'd better get Mackereth back. I won't show them." She stalked straight up to Hill Top and into mother's kitchen and said, "I'll tell you what it is, Mrs Storey, your husband's a bad tempered little devil." She just said that and walked out, and there was no more said.'

There was also a ram among the Hill Top Herdwicks which Tom recognised as one he had himself picked out as a winner when it was a lamb at Eskdale Show and which had done well since, so that was a good start to the breeding programme. He also picked out two lambs with which he won prizes for Mrs Heelis at Hawkshead Show that autumn. 'Eh, she was pleased. I said I was glad for that and hoped we win a few more.' This proved to be the case. Hill Top Herdwicks won prizes at all the shows, Keswick, Ennerdale, Eskdale, Loweswater, as well as the local ones, from then on until the outbreak of the Second World War, and had an

Right: *Beatrix Potter at Hawkshead Show*

Previous page: *The countryside around Hawkshead and Sawrey*
Above: *Re-roofing a Trust cottage*

unbeaten record with ewes from 1930 until 1939. Mrs
Heelis won silver tea sets, salvers, vases and tankards – and
she always gave the tankards to Tom.

As she acquired more farms, Mrs Heelis had increased
her flocks of Herdwicks. She had a great pride in these little
sheep, but worried over them in bad weather. 'This is such a
bad time for the sheep,' she wrote to the Banners in the
winter of 1937. 'The snow storm that was so severe in the
south missed us – or delayed – till last Sunday, when there
was the heaviest fall for twenty years; and it thaws so very
slowly; freezing under the bright moon again. Perhaps it is a
superstition that the moon causes frost; effect, not cause. We
feed them here, but they don't thrive on hay and it's impos-

sible to feed a big fell flock. Old customs become disused. I have just been telling the men to cut some 'croppit ashes'. That is why you see the surviving croppit ashes near fell farmhouses. It used to be the custom to crop ashes and hollies for the sheep.'

However, even when engrossed with sheep-breeding Mrs Heelis was never too busy to help the National Trust. In 1927 there came a particularly urgent appeal for money. A strip of the shore of Windermere on the east side of the lake near the ferry was to come up for sale. It was sure to be bought by a builder as prime land for 'superior' houses, unless the Trust could raise the purchase money in time to prevent this despoliation and save a little of Windermere shore for public access.

Mrs Heelis was short of money, farming being in its usual doldrums, and she failed to persuade her mother there was any need to prevent the ownership of all lake shores being in private hands. It then occurred to her that she might raise a little money by selling some of her own drawings, perhaps in America where for some reason that seemed inexplicable to her she was regarded as an important literary figure.

The editor of the *Horn Book Magazine*, Miss Bertha Mahony, who had written asking for particulars of Beatrix Potter, was startled to receive fifty signed copies of drawings of Peter Rabbit with the request she should sell them on behalf of Beatrix Potter to raise money for the preservation of a piece of the Lake District, price one guinea (£1 1s.) each. As Miss Mahony also ran the Bookshop for Boys and Girls in Boston, the drawings soon sold, there were requests for more, and the final sum raised was £104.

Mrs Heelis was most impressed with the kindness of the Americans and in her letter of thanks she expanded on the need for preserving the English countryside. It was, she told them, only a matter of time before educational advances would ensure the proper appreciation of unspoilt nature; it would be a great pity if that appreciation came too late.

The correspondence with American friends continued. Anne Carroll Moore, Superintendent of Children's Work in the New York Public Library, had visited Mrs Heelis in June 1921 and made a good impression. She recommended other literary people who called when in England, so eventually a coterie of friends was formed on the other side of the Atlantic. Most probably, when they came to Sawrey, they were entertained to tea at Hill Top. Mrs Heelis's married life, where she put a basket of apples on the back porch for the blackbirds to peck and warmed William's slippers against his homecoming, was in another world, and at Hill Top even these friendly people were safely away from it. She kept a few rabbits in a run on the grass in the garden. 'I keep rabbits so that children will not be disappointed,' she once told Josephine. She was greatly pleased that children who came to see her expected to find all her little creatures to be living with her – particularly Peter Rabbit.

It was in one of her letters to America in 1929 that Mrs Heelis mentioned having been driven by William to Coniston on a lovely evening to look at some land for sale in which the National Trust was interested. The autumn colours had been glorious.

Letters continued, and soon the news from Westmorland was that Mrs Heelis had been made President of the

Herdwick Sheepbreeders' Association. She seemed to take the honour in her stride, finding humour in a situation where she, a total abstainer, attended meetings of the association with other farmers in a tavern after a sheep sale or show.

It was the first time there had been a women president in the history of the association, founded by Canon Rawnsley and his son Noel, and Mrs Heelis took the work seriously, particularly judging. She once told friends, appointed to meet her at Eskdale Show, not to speak to her until the afternoon when all business was over. A greatly respected figure, she went round the pens dressed always in a Herdwick tweed suit and severe brown felt hat. She always said she could not be doing with a hat that blew off; this one was secured with black elastic under her chin.

Tom Storey was required to attend shows with his employer and relates that when it came to going into the Members' Tent for lunch the ritual was always the same. She would turn to Tom and say, 'I think you'll be wanting to get home, won't you Storey?' He would reply, 'Yes, I'd like to be going back' – and then the two of them would go off and have lunch in a little teashop round the corner. 'That was more in her line; she was really shy, you know.'

Association dinners had to be attended, and American friends were told the story of a jolly farmer who, in proposing a toast to the president, compared her to a cow – with very neat legs – which had just won a first prize. Mrs Heelis thought she was less like a cow and more like a good-tempered witch – or perhaps a fairy godmother.

Mrs Heelis had in fact already taken on the role of Fairy

Godmother to the National Trust. She had bought the Monk Coniston Estate, inspected with William on that autumn evening, which included among much else Tarn Hows, Tom Heights, Tilberthwaite, Yewdale and the summit of Wetherlam. She had then offered to sell half of it, 2,600 acres (1,050 ha), to the Trust at cost price, to be paid for as and when it could be done. There was also the promise that the remainder of the estate would eventually come to the Trust as well. The money was raised quickly with the help of local benefactors, but Mrs Heelis was asked to continue to manage it for the Trust. Mr S.H. Hamer, the Secretary of the Trust, thought she should do so at least for the time being. Land owned by the Trust in the Lake District at that time was managed by local committees who were lacking in agricultural experience. Mrs Heelis took the job.

This increase of responsibilities was met with a sort of brisk, matter-of-fact zest. The usual repair and planning problems of a land agent – an amateur land agent was how she saw herself – were much complicated by the world Depression.

At the 1932 autumn sheep sales in Westmorland some animals were sold for as little as one shilling. Tenants asked for reductions in rent. Mrs Heelis met these requests with sympathy but had to make her own economies when repairs were needed. Workmen were taken over to Yewdale in the 'Noah's Ark', Mrs Heelis's old car, to keep bills down; real need was distinguished from mere grumbling when it came to damp walls and faulty drains. She found drains most interesting, noting for future managers that Thwaite had a fine main drain but that the man who built it had lost his level about fifteen yards in. She had had the sides of the sewer raised to give more head-room, but expected it to silt up as time went on.

The work of a land agent was not the only extra concern. Mrs Heelis had been pushed into being an author again – temporarily – by an American publisher: a longer book illustrated mostly with drawings had been commissioned, and work had to be done each day. 'In fine weather you'd see her go across', Tom Storey said. 'She had a wicket gate put in the field to go to Hill Top. She'd do her writing in good weather on the highest point of the pasture. In wet weather she'd be in the house.'

Tom was asked for his help. 'She came across and she said, "Storey, the next lamb that dies, could you cut its head off for me and skin it back to the shoulder?"' He did as she asked. The next time he came down the lane to look at a sheep he saw her sitting on a stone in the field, sketching the head which was fastened to the wall.

The Fairy Caravan, really a book of short stories, was published in America, and Tom Storey was presented with a signed copy. After more persuasion Mrs Heelis put together *Little Pig Robinson*, which was published in 1930. This completed, she was able to return to farming interests with the satisfactory feeling she had fulfilled all demands.

Sheep prices were improving by 1934, the situation was better all round, and there were 700 sheep to draft out of the flocks. In 1935 sheep bred by Tom Storey won many prizes, including a silver cup won outright (third time) for a Champion Herdwick Ewe. By this time electricity had come to Sawrey, generally welcomed, but Mrs Heelis preferred the

soft light of oil lamps and candles. 'I'll put it in the shippon,' she said. 'The cows may like it.'

The Storeys would have liked electricity in the farm, but Tom Storey emphasised she was good to work for. 'She never ordered me what to do. I used to take the milk to Castle Farm every morning, she was always there to meet me, at the door, just before 8, she was a good getter up, and she'd say "Well?" and I'd say well I'm going to do so and so today. That's all that was said. It was all right by her. Oh, we got on well. I wouldn't have stayed here for twenty years if we didn't.'

In 1936 the National Trust appointed Bruce Thompson to be their agent in the Lake District. The time of caretaking was over for Mrs Heelis but the transfer of responsibility was no light task. It was not just a case of turning over the management of the farms to the agent, but the method of management as well. The opening of a regional office did not mean it was an immediately efficient estate office: Mrs Heelis did her best to help it become one.

Lists of workmen she had employed for the many repairs that had been necessary were supplied, together with their individual strengths and weaknesses. Cookson was recommended for roofs and for Rose Castle as he knew about the key. She also laboured to impart some elementary knowledge of agricultural matters to Mr Thompson, whom she thought young for the job, emphasising the necessity to use round wire near flood water as wire netting could get clogged with drift, and warning him that he should not be put off with anything thinner than size 9, remembering that 10 is thinner and 8 is thicker.

Previous page: *Penny Hill Farm, Eskdale*. Right: *Little Langdale*

They worried together about problems of public access to Trust land. Bathing in Tarn Hows caused much heart-searching, but finally it was decided to allow it though well away from the road. Mrs Heelis was of the opinion that rules were difficult, particularly after having seen some local people waltzing on the ice to the music of a gramophone. She thought a general habit of gramophoning and wireless-ing would be a great nuisance.

Mrs Heelis was worried about Trust management. This was the first time the National Trust had been faced with estate work; would they prove responsible, or would the land and properties be allowed to decay again? Well, time would tell. Mrs Heelis dusted her hands of the problem for the moment and went back to her own farming with a little more time to look round.

She was trying to find her friends the Banners somewhere to live among the fells, and she wrote to them about the Elterwater estate, noting at the same time that there had been lovely days above the fog with frosty sunsets behind Wetherlam. A few letters later she was telling them she was not too proud to go up to Heathwaite in a milk float provided they could haul her into it. She had accepted the invitation that was to offer the experience of seeing herself, past, present and future, from the centre of her own world.

REQUIEM

Mrs Heelis died on 22 December 1943, having lived long enough to know that the war, whose shadow was already looking dark when she took the milk float up to Heathwaite, was being won by the Allies. The ownership of her beloved land would not pass into alien hands. The last time the Banners saw her she had looked very small and pretty and, like Timmy Willie, she had waved goodbye from the little gate, smiling with her head on one side and waving a clover leaf she had just picked. Delmar Banner's portrait of Mrs Heelis at the age of seventy-two at Keswick Show hangs at the Beatrix Pottery Gallery in Hawkeshead; a replica is in the National Portrait Gallery.

Tom Storey had been shocked at her death – 'because I'd been talking to her an hour or more the night before, about the farm and everything.' He had been charged with the duty of scattering her ashes on Hill Top pastures. 'She said, whatever I did, to tell nobody.'

The farming world of Cumberland and Westmorland agreed with the shepherd who remarked 'Aye, it's a bad day for farmers' at her funeral. The Trust, too, had lost a friend. Her help and advice as a councillor – sometimes a nannie – had been invaluable.

In her will Mrs Heelis had left the Trust the rest of the Monk Coniston estate, together with all her other farms, land and cottages, including Hill Top. The intervening years had given the Trust time to prove its good faith and ability, and though Mrs Heelis considered there were weaknesses – too lenient with tenants – she had been finally convinced the National Trust had the best interests of the Lake District at heart. In all, the bequest amounted to 4,000 acres (1,620 ha) and many properties, a most important gift not only for the actual number of acres but for what it represented. Mrs Heelis's concern to protect dale heads, prevent road widening in vulnerable valleys and keep small cottages, barns and other vernacular buildings intact for the part they played in the pattern of the landscape, were aims and ideals passed on to become Trust policy for the Lake District as a whole.

The Trust now owns a quarter of the Lake District National Park, around 140,000 acres (56,660 ha) of land. The farms bought by Mrs Heelis are among the ninety-one managed by the Regional Office. Sheep belonging to the Trust total about 25,000, many of them the little Herdwicks she found so admirable a breed. There is also an estate staff of builders, foresters and wardens which Bruce Thompson could well have envied, but the same aims and principles that guided him also guide the land agents – beautiful countryside must be protected for the benefit of the nation.

Among the 140,000 acres are some of the most spectacular areas of the Lake District, but also to be found are the gentle hills, rolling pastures and small tarns of the countryside round Hawkshead and Sawrey, with the whitewashed farmhouses and cottages a pleasure to the eye. This was Beatrix Potter's gift to the nation, her own beloved countryside for all to enjoy – the real world of Beatrix Potter.